# inside story

Tony D Triggs

Book 3

**Acknowledgements**

Ace Photo Agency.

Ancient Art and Architecture Collection.

Barnaby's Picture Library.

BBC Hulton Picture Library.

Bridgeman Art Library.

Jane Burton/Bruce Coleman Ltd.

Daily Telegraph Colour Library/Space Frontiers.

Mary Evans Picture Library.

Mary Evans/Fawcett Library.

Michael Holford.

International Centre for Conservation Education.

Marion and Tony Morrison.

Oxford Scientific Films Ltd.

Rex Features.

Seaphot Ltd: Planet Earth Pictures.

Scott Polar Research Institute.

# Contents

| | |
|---|---|
| The Secrets of El Dorado | 4 |
| Walking Tall | 9 |
| Sources of Power | 10 |
| Hats that Sold Ice Cream | 13 |
| All Fall Down | 14 |
| The Great Fire | 16 |
| The Story of the Suffragettes | 20 |
| Bees that Dance | 25 |
| Is There Anyone There? | 26 |
| Adventure in Antarctica | 28 |

# THE SECRETS OF EL DORADO

In the 16th century explorers from Europe searched for a city they called El Dorado. They thought it was in the northern part of South America. Their task was extremely hard, for most of the land was covered in jungle. They had to use axes to cut through the tangled creepers and branches. Snakes and dangerous insects attacked them, and sometimes they had to wade through swamps where greedy alligators lurked.

Hidden away in this unexplored land there were fields and villages. These were the homes of Indian people known as Incas. The Incas had lived in peace for many hundreds of years. They worshipped the sun and made beautiful jewellery out of gold.

The explorers wanted the gold for themselves. They plundered the villages, wrecking the huts and killing the people. The explorers wanted to know where the Incas' gold mines were; they also wanted to find and rob El Dorado and other wealthy towns. The Incas said they got their gold by trading with others. They said they had never heard of a place called El Dorado.

The explorers were sure El Dorado existed, and some of them thought it was built of gold. This was because they came from Spain and they knew what El Dorado meant: it was Spanish for *The Golden One*. No wonder they were eager to find it!

Gonzalo Quesada was one of the people who searched for the city. He led a party of 500 soldiers into the jungle. They journeyed for months, and most of them died of snake-bites and fever. Quesada could see that the others were dying of hunger and tiredness. Sometimes they chewed their belts in their sleep because they were starving.

One day they saw a distant town which gleamed like the sun. It was on a bare hillside which rose from the jungle. Greedy for gold and desperate for food, the men climbed the hill and attacked the town. Most of the Incas fled when they saw these savage thugs. Some tried to use their poisoned arrows; others were killed by the Spaniards' swords or taken as prisoners.

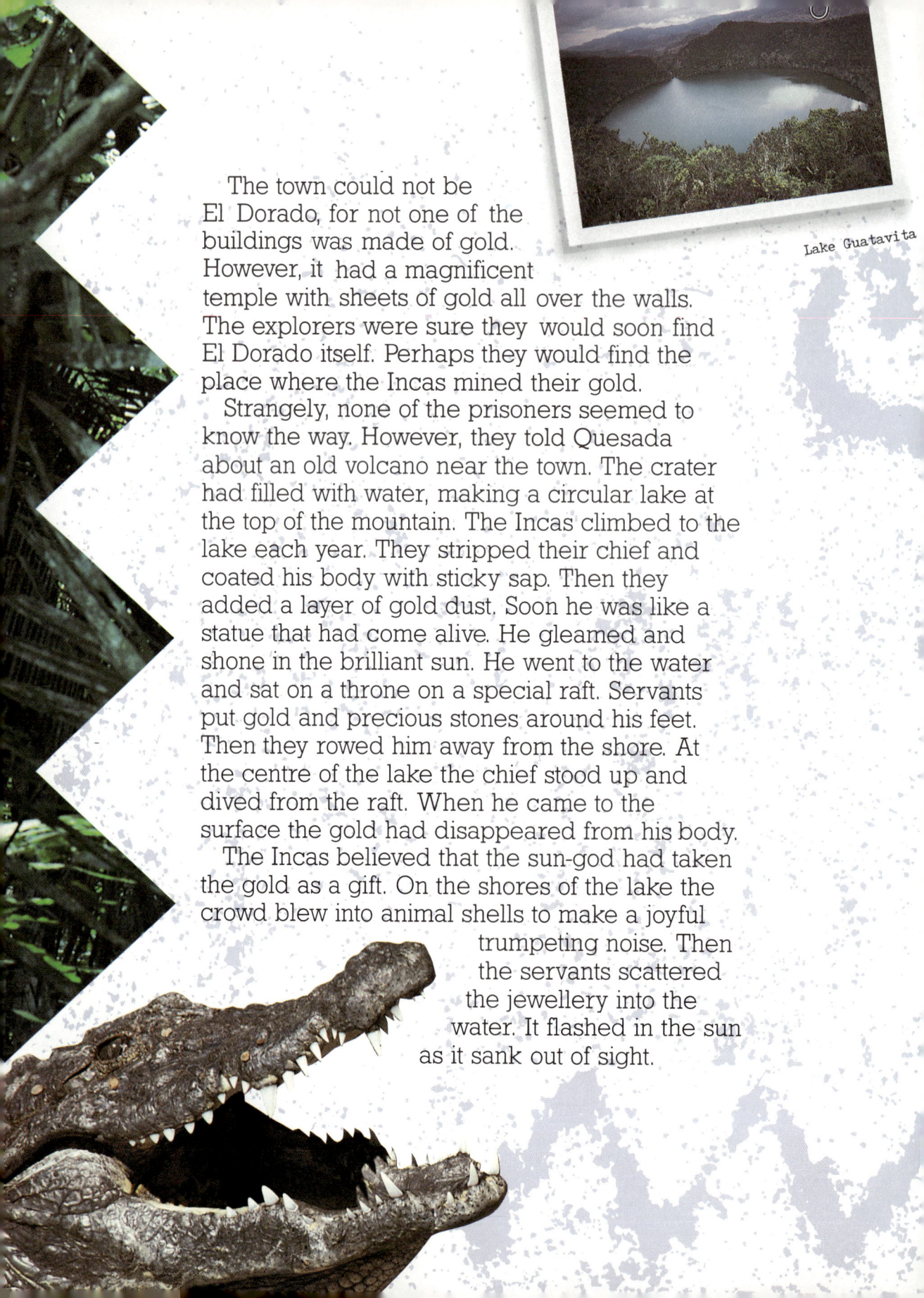

The town could not be El Dorado, for not one of the buildings was made of gold. However, it had a magnificent temple with sheets of gold all over the walls. The explorers were sure they would soon find El Dorado itself. Perhaps they would find the place where the Incas mined their gold.

Strangely, none of the prisoners seemed to know the way. However, they told Quesada about an old volcano near the town. The crater had filled with water, making a circular lake at the top of the mountain. The Incas climbed to the lake each year. They stripped their chief and coated his body with sticky sap. Then they added a layer of gold dust. Soon he was like a statue that had come alive. He gleamed and shone in the brilliant sun. He went to the water and sat on a throne on a special raft. Servants put gold and precious stones around his feet. Then they rowed him away from the shore. At the centre of the lake the chief stood up and dived from the raft. When he came to the surface the gold had disappeared from his body.

The Incas believed that the sun-god had taken the gold as a gift. On the shores of the lake the crowd blew into animal shells to make a joyful trumpeting noise. Then the servants scattered the jewellery into the water. It flashed in the sun as it sank out of sight.

Lake Guatavita

This was a sign that the god was pleased.

Quesada wanted the gold for himself, so he led his men to the holy lake. They could see some empty huts on the shore, but that was all. They started to scoop the water out with buckets and cups. Slowly the lake got lower and smaller. Soon they found some little gold statues in the mud. However, they knew that most of the treasure would be in the deepest part of the lake. Quesada wanted to empty all the water out, but lightning killed him before he could try. Some people thought that the gods had done it because they were angry.

After his death another man tried to reach the treasure. He and his workers cut a gap in the side of the crater. The water spilled down the side of the mountain, and lots of treasure was found in the mud. However, some rocks fell into the gap and blocked it before the crater was empty. The accident killed two or three of the workers and frightened the rest. There was still a deep pool in the middle of the crater, but no one dared to try again for many years.

Gold model of Inca chief on raft

At last, at the start of this century, an English firm pumped all the water out of the crater. However, the sun was very hot and it baked the mud as hard as concrete. As a result, very little was found. Then rain filled the crater up again!

The treasure is still in the lake today. The mountain is in Colombia, and the country has made new laws to stop people hunting for treasure.

However, twenty years ago two Colombian farmers discovered a tiny cave in the hills. They peered inside and saw something glinting. It was a beautiful model made of gold and it showed an Inca chief and his servants on their raft.

No one will ever find the city of El Dorado. It does not exist and it never did. Explorers were making a bad mistake when they thought that El Dorado was a golden place. *The Golden One* was really a person — the Inca chief with his coating of gold dust.

# Walking Tall

**D**id you know that important people like to be taller than everyone else? Often they try to make themselves tall by wearing crowns or special hats. If they cannot do that they can choose a hairstyle that makes them look taller. For example, they can brush their hair to make it stand up.

Some people want to seem more important than they are. These people often have very fierce hairstyles.

Monks do not want to feel important. They want to feel humble. Because of this they cut off most or all of their hair. Without their hair they seem a lot shorter. They look weak and humble, and this helps to stop them feeling proud.

People can bow or curtsey or kneel to make themselves seem shorter or lower. They do it in front of important people. It helps the important people to feel really mighty and grand. Thrones and platforms help them too!

Gentlemen sometimes remove their hats to be polite. They do it because it makes them seem shorter. They are trying to say that the other person is really more important than they are. Some men raise their hats instead. They are trying to be polite, of course, but in a way they are being rude. They are making themselves look taller, not shorter! Like other people, they don't understand the signals we give with our hair and our bodies.

## Sources of Power

How do we get electricity? Much of it comes from power stations which burn oil or coal. However, the coal and oil in the world will not last forever. Most people think they will run out next century.

Perhaps we should get our electricity in other ways. Nowadays, many countries are building nuclear power stations. These do not need coal or oil but they need a sort of metal called uranium. Uranium comes from special mines. It is a dangerous substance which has to be treated very carefully. People who work with it sometimes get an illness called cancer.

In 1986 at Chernobyl in the USSR there was a very serious accident at a nuclear power station. It showed the world how dangerous this form of power could be.

A nuclear power station

Wind power

What about natural sources of power, such as waves and wind?

The wind can be very powerful indeed. Think of the damage a gale can do! People have used the wind to drive windmills for hundreds of years. The machinery can grind up grain. It can also be used for pumping water or working dynamos. These can provide electricity for other jobs. However, a windmill can only provide a little power; and if the wind stops the windmill stops too!

Some people fix special panels onto the roofs of their houses. These turn the power of the sun into electricity for heating. This is called solar power. However, the sun shines less in winter, and this is when people need energy most.

Perhaps we should use the power of the sea. Waves can turn rocks into grains of sand. They can wear away cliffs and destroy the towns that were built on top. Maybe the power in the waves can be turned into electricity.

Solar power

Wave power

Kariba Dam

Tides can be even more powerful than waves. Twice every day the sea rises and falls. It can rise and fall by as much as three metres. There are parts of the world where the difference is even greater than this. Millions of tonnes of sea-water run in and out of river mouths every day of the year. A dam has been built across the mouth of a river in France. The water runs backwards and forwards through special gaps in the dam. As it goes through the gaps it works gigantic dynamos (called generators).

Inland rivers are also used to generate electricity. Look at the picture and try to decide why rivers in mountains are best for this.

# Hats that Sold Ice Cream

One hundred years ago, many men wore bowler hats. To be polite, they would raise their hats when they greeted their neighbours. This was rather hard to do if their hands were full. Someone decided to solve this problem. He invented a gadget that raised hats automatically. The user nodded — and up went the hat till the brim was as high as the top of his head. It spun round once and settled into place again.

Before every outing the user had to fit the gadget into his hat and wind it up. When he put the hat on, some springy fingers gripped his head. Now he knew that his twirling hat was ready for action!

Some people thought that the gadget was just a foolish joke; the inventor said that traders would pay to put their advertisements on his hat. As it twizzled round it would tell people where to buy the best ice cream! Well-off people would not want advertisements on their hats, but poor folk could earn themselves money like this.

In 1912, someone found a simpler way of making a hat go up and down. The wearer needed a rubber bulb which he could squeeze. A tube from the bulb went up his arm to an empty balloon underneath his hat. Squeezing the bulb sent air through the tube. It filled the balloon — and up went the hat!

# All Fall Down

*Ring a ring o' roses,*
*A pocket full of posies,*
*Atishoo! Atishoo!*
*We all fall down.*

**F**ew people know that this rhyme is really about a disease called the plague. Lots of people used to die of it. In 1349 it killed nearly half the people in Europe. Often, the victims dropped dead in the streets. Other people were frightened of catching the plague themselves, so they left the bodies where they fell.

Cities were filthy places to live in. Cattle were sometimes kept in the streets. Near butchers' shops the cobbles were often slippery with dung, and the air was full of evil smells and the buzzing of flies.

Nowadays we can turn a tap and get plenty of water to make things clean. In those days water came from wells. It was often brown and bad to drink, but drinking from rivers was even worse, for people poured their sewage and filth straight into the water.

Merchants used horses and carts to carry their goods to the markets; the rich had horse-drawn coaches to take them to parties and plays. Nowadays, cars and lorries poison the air with fumes, so horse-drawn vehicles were probably better for people's health. However, in the busier streets the horse-dung was often ankle deep, and the smell was foul.

People knew that dirt and filth helped

diseases to spread, but they could not make their cities clean. Everyone crowded together like insects; no one could change the way so many people lived.

Some Londoners tried to stop the evil smells from going up their noses. They did this by carrying bunches of sweetly scented flowers. They held them as close to their faces as possible.

The nursery rhyme was written hundreds of years ago, and some of the words are hard to understand today. A posy can be a bunch of flowers or herbs, or the words on a lucky charm. If you study the second line of the rhyme you can probably guess what the writer meant.

The first line is also rather mysterious. However, we know that people with plague had rings of rose-coloured spots on their bodies. Perhaps the writer was thinking of these.

The last two lines of the rhyme are less puzzling. After the spots appeared on their bodies the victims often began to sneeze; and a day or two later they fell down dead.

Did you know that plague is still a killer disease? It is found in parts of Asia and Africa. The last attack in Britain occurred this century. It affected some Suffolk villages from 1906 to 1918. Twenty-two villagers caught the disease and most of them died.

# Great Of L

Samuel Pepys was born in 1633. He worked for King Charles II and he had a large house in Seething Lane near the Tower of London.

Pepys is famous today because of the interesting diary he wrote. The Great Fire of London, which happened in 1666, is one of the things he wrote about. He described how his maids had woken him up to tell him that nearby houses were burning. Pepys's house was built of brick, but much of London was crowded with houses and shops made of wood. Pepys looked out of his window and saw that clusters of houses were already blazing. Other houses were getting hot and starting to smoke. The wind was taking the smoke and fire away from Pepys's house towards the centre of London. How much of the city would be destroyed?

As soon as the sun came up Pepys dressed. He went to the Tower and he climbed the stone staircase in one of the turrets. He looked from

# The Fire of London

the top at the blazing streets. The fire had reached the banks of the Thames, and sheds full of oil and candle-wax were exploding like bombs. Even the houses on London Bridge were burning now, and walls were falling into the river. Pepys could see the steaming wreckage floating beneath him past the Tower.

Pepys dashed down the stairs and went to the river. He needed to see the King at once so he called to a man who carried passengers in his boat. He asked the man to take him up the river to Whitehall.

They had to go under London Bridge, where many houses were still ablaze. Pepys felt the scorching heat of the flames. He saw pigeons fall from the Bridge because their wings had been burned.

At Whitehall Pepys went to see King Charles. He told the King that the fire would never stop by itself. They would have to pull some houses down before the fire reached them.

The gap in the houses would stop the fire spreading. The King agreed with Pepys's idea. He said that the Mayor of London was trying to deal with the fire. He told Pepys to find him and ask him to start pulling houses down.

Pepys set off through the narrow streets, but he had to go slowly. The smoke in the sky made everything gloomy, and frightened people were trying to run away from the fire.

When Pepys found the Mayor he told him to start pulling houses down.

"We've been doing that," the Mayor replied, "but the fire overtakes us faster than we can pull them down."

That night the glare of the fire shone in through all Pepys's windows. He knew he would have to leave the house, but perhaps he could save his possessions first. Pepys and his wife spent a very hot night taking chests full of money down the stairs to the cellar. Pepys also buried some bags of gold and boxes of papers in the garden. At daybreak he loaded a cart with his diary and some of his other favourite possessions and sent them away to a house in the country.

Two nights later, the fire reached the end of Seething Lane, so Pepys and his wife escaped by boat. At daybreak Pepys went back to see if his house was in flames. However, he found that men with explosives had blown up the rows of wooden houses ahead of the fire. This was faster than pulling them down, and had stopped the fire from reaching the gunpowder stored in the Tower. It had also stopped it from reaching Pepys's magnificent house!

However, the fire could not be stopped on every side. It carried on burning for several days, till most of the ancient city was gone and 13,000 people were homeless.

The fire had caused great fear and suffering. However, it did some good things too. It meant that a man called Christopher Wren could design fine new churches in place of the old ones. The finest of all was his new cathedral. People who visit St Paul's today should thank Sir Christopher Wren — and the fire.

The fire also helped to deal with the filth and overcrowding in London. This had caused a lot of disease. For example, a bad attack of plague had only just ended. Now the old, unhealthy houses had been destroyed. New ones were built, and these were usually larger and cleaner. As a result, plague and other diseases became less common in London.

# The Story of the Suffragettes

"We drove to No. 10 Downing Street... and threw our stones through the window panes. As expected, we were promptly arrested... At intervals of 15 minutes, other women did their work, smashing glass in the Haymarket and Piccadilly..., splintering glass along Regent Street and the Strand..., breaking the windows in Oxford Circus and Broad Street."

Eighty years ago things like this were quite common in Britain. The women who did them were angry about the unfair laws which stopped women voting in national elections. The right to vote is sometimes called suffrage, and people called these angry women suffragettes.

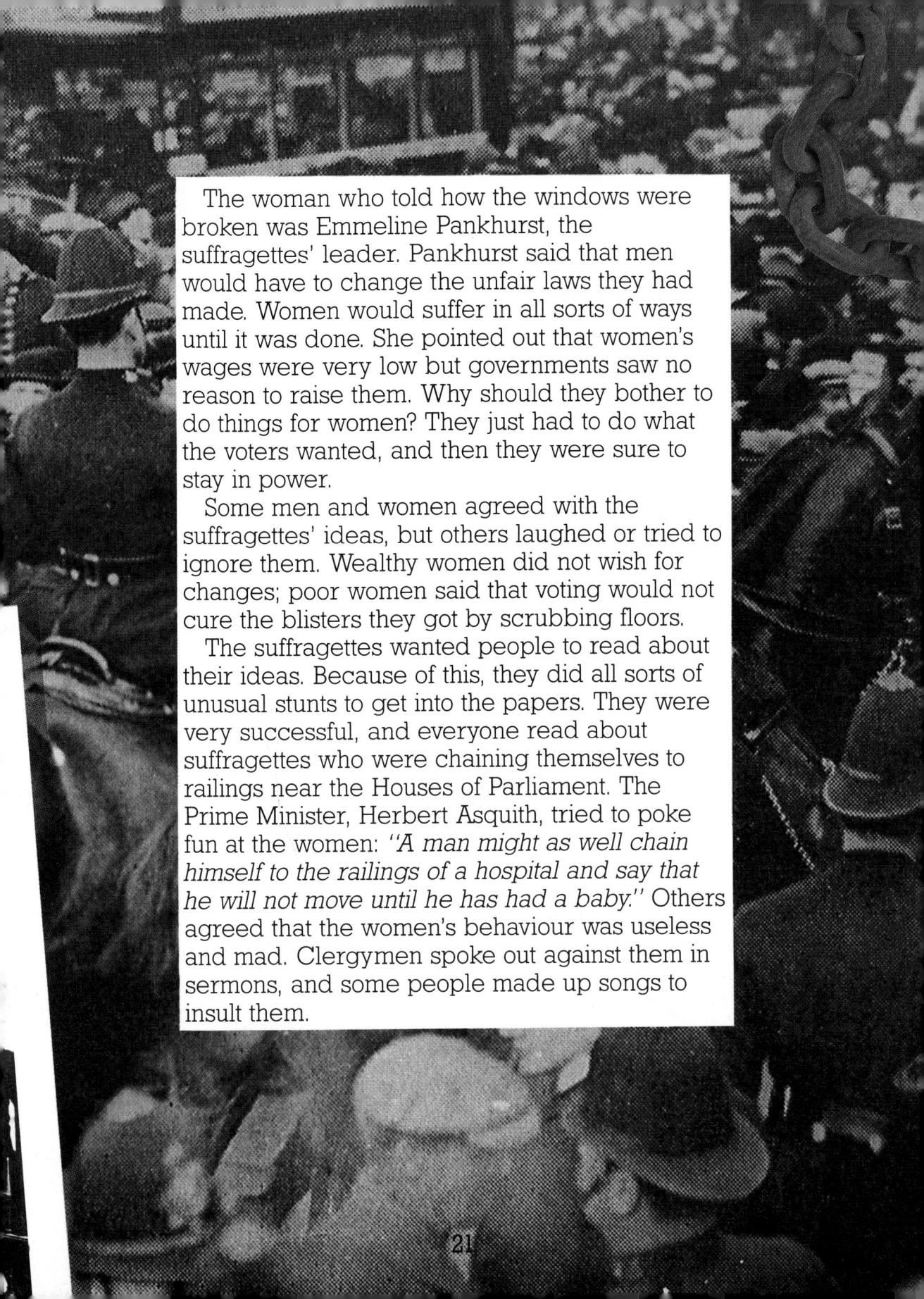

The woman who told how the windows were broken was Emmeline Pankhurst, the suffragettes' leader. Pankhurst said that men would have to change the unfair laws they had made. Women would suffer in all sorts of ways until it was done. She pointed out that women's wages were very low but governments saw no reason to raise them. Why should they bother to do things for women? They just had to do what the voters wanted, and then they were sure to stay in power.

Some men and women agreed with the suffragettes' ideas, but others laughed or tried to ignore them. Wealthy women did not wish for changes; poor women said that voting would not cure the blisters they got by scrubbing floors.

The suffragettes wanted people to read about their ideas. Because of this, they did all sorts of unusual stunts to get into the papers. They were very successful, and everyone read about suffragettes who were chaining themselves to railings near the Houses of Parliament. The Prime Minister, Herbert Asquith, tried to poke fun at the women: *"A man might as well chain himself to the railings of a hospital and say that he will not move until he has had a baby."* Others agreed that the women's behaviour was useless and mad. Clergymen spoke out against them in sermons, and some people made up songs to insult them.

Force-feeding

The suffragettes refused to give up. They went on marches, handed out leaflets and gave rousing speeches. They also went to meetings where men were going to speak. Sometimes they got there first and hid underneath the platform. Then they popped out when the meeting began. This was their chance to say what they thought!

Suffragettes were often arrested and put into prison. Some suffragettes refused to eat any prison food. They knew that this would make things very hard for the government. People would call them murderers if the women died. To keep them alive the prison doctors fed them by force, but people said that this was too brutal. In the end, the government decided to let the women go without their prison food. However, when they were very weak the prison authorities sent them home to get strong again. Then they took them back to jail. This often happened several times before a woman's sentence was over. Like everything else, it made people cross with the government's methods. Some people wanted the women to starve but most people felt that the treatment was cruel.

Some suffragettes went home to recover but then disappeared. The police used to wait for the missing women at suffragette rallies. As soon as they went on the stage to speak the policemen pounced. The women were pleased because cameras clicked and another report appeared in the papers.

The suffragettes did not like hurting other people. However, they found that politicians promised them things then broke their word. Because of this they began to smash windows in shops and offices. They also set fire to public buildings like churches and stations.

What else could women do to be noticed? In 1913 a suffragette called Emily Davidson went to a horse race known as the Derby. One of the horses belonged to the King and Davidson threw herself under its hooves as it galloped along.

Davidson had given her life. Her funeral was front page news and most people thought that the government would soon give in to the suffragettes.

Davidson throws herself under the King's horse

23

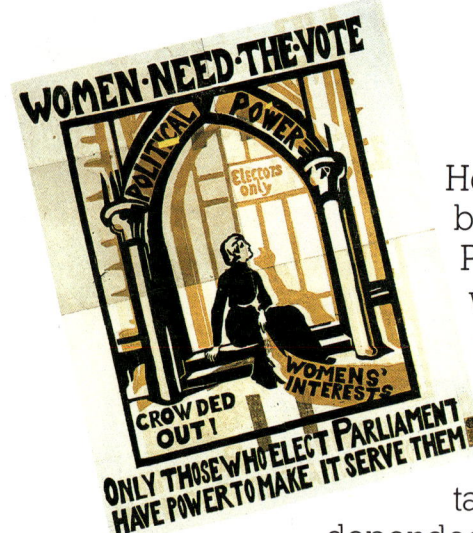

However, the First World War began in the following year. Mrs Pankhurst felt that winning the war was more important than anything else. She told the suffragettes to stop all the things they were doing. Young men were going away to fight, and women had to take over their jobs. The nation depended on women now, and everyone felt they deserved the right to vote like men.

The fighting ended in 1918. Soldiers came home, and some told of nurses and other brave women who risked their lives to save people in danger. Stories like this made the nation more eager to let women vote. A new law was made by the end of the year. This allowed women to vote when they reached the age of 30. Ten years later the law was changed so that women could vote at 21 (the same as men).

Mrs Pankhurst was old and ill and she died soon after the change was made. However, she knew that her struggle for women's rights had succeeded.

Women making tanks during the war

# Bees that Dance

**B**ees cannot talk so they dance instead. They do this to let each other know where food can be found.

A dancing bee begins by running in a straight line. As she runs she waggles her body to make the other bees look. At the end of the run she turns to the left and hurries back to where she began. She does her wiggly run again, but this time she turns to the right at the end. She is making a sort of figure of eight. (You can use your finger to see where the bee in the diagram goes. She will probably go round dozens of times before she stops.)

A bee may dance in front of the hive or she may go inside. If so, she will have to dance on the upright face of the honeycomb. The wiggly run is the part of the dance which tells the others where to go for nectar. If the bee runs straight up the face of the comb the others must fly towards the sun. If she goes just a little to the left or the right the others must fly just a little to the left or the right of the sun. Which way do you think the others must fly if the bee runs *down* the honeycomb?

The dancer can even tell the others how far away the food is. A long wiggly run means that the food is a long way away. A short wiggly run means that the food is very close. Sometimes a bee goes round and round without any wiggly bits at all. That means the food is by the hive.

# Is There Anyone There?

Is there life on other planets? One hundred years ago people thought that the answer was 'yes'. Astronomers studied the planet Mars with telescopes, and some of them said they could see canals. Maybe these carried water to the Martians' crops!

Then the astronomers changed their minds about the canals. They began to use better telescopes, and all they could see were mountains and valleys. They found that the planet was dry and cold, with very little air to breathe. It seemed unlikely that creatures could live there after all.

Mars and the Earth are two of the planets that go round the sun. Other planets go round the sun too, but they probably do not have any life. Some are too hot for living things and the rest are too cold.

Voyager spacecraft

Surface of Mars

Metal plate carried by spacecraft

    Maybe people were wrong about life on other worlds. However, there are millions of stars, and some of them have their own sets of planets. This means that there are lots of places where life could exist.

    How can we get in touch with any creatures who live there? Scientists listen for radio messages coming from space, and they try sending messages of their own. They also send spacecraft towards the stars. There is no one on board, since the journey will take many thousands of years. Instead, the crafts carry metal plates. They show what human beings are like, and they also show where the spacecraft has come from.

    Alien creatures may one day see a spacecraft from Earth flying over their heads. Perhaps they will know how to bring it down safely. Then perhaps they will study the pictures and think about sending a message to Earth.

# Adventure in Antarctica

In 1914 a party of twenty-eight men sailed to the frozen land of Antarctica. They wanted to walk right across it. However, the sea froze all around their ship before they could land. The sides of the ship were made of wood and soon they began to creak and groan, for the ice was pressing hard against them. It was crushing the ship, but the men could do nothing about it. Now they would have to survive in tents on the frozen sea. Without their ship they were trapped in Antarctica.

They camped on the ice for nearly a month, and they saw how it crunched their ship into pieces. Then the ice parted, and most of the wreckage sank to the bottom.

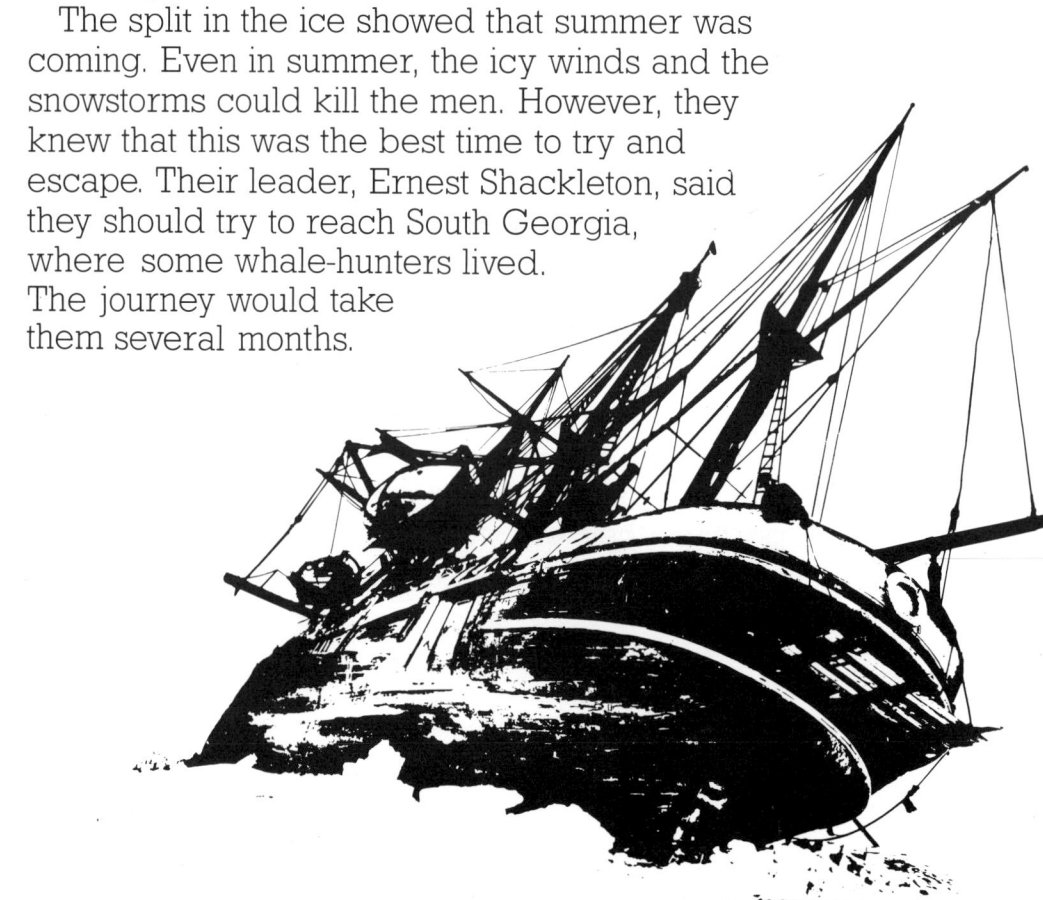

The split in the ice showed that summer was coming. Even in summer, the icy winds and the snowstorms could kill the men. However, they knew that this was the best time to try and escape. Their leader, Ernest Shackleton, said they should try to reach South Georgia, where some whale-hunters lived. The journey would take them several months.

If they ran out of food they could try to kill seals.

They had saved three lifeboats from the ship, so they filled them with stores and tied them onto sledges. Then they harnessed dogs to the sledges and set off across the frozen sea.

The men walked for weeks without finding any seals to eat. In the end they had to eat their dogs. They were short of fuel so they ate the dogs raw. They rarely had anything hot to drink. They melted mugs of ice by putting them under their clothes. Then they drank the water cold.

During the summer the men got weaker and weaker. They had to pull the sledges themselves, but the boats were very heavy indeed. The men knew the ice was getting thin, and the weight of the sledges could easily break it. Soon it was breaking up by itself, and islands of ice were floating away.

The men got onto one of these islands. They knew that they were risking their lives, for it might split up into smaller parts. Then they could drown or whales might attack them. However, they knew that the ice was drifting away from Antarctica. It was like a raft and it saved them from walking. Storms might force them to stay in their tents for many days. Even so, they were still on the move!

Sometimes they used their boats to get from one sheet of ice to another one. Then they decided to row to an island called Elephant Island.

After several days the starving men saw the Island ahead. There was spray breaking over the barren rocks, but they managed to land. There were plenty of seals and seaweed to eat, but they needed to get to South Georgia soon. Winter was coming, and some of the men might die if they stayed on Elephant Island. However, they knew that the stormy seas might drown them if they tried to leave.

Shackleton said that a few of the men should risk their lives to get help for the others. They should try to reach South Georgia in one of the boats. He was willing to go in the boat himself but he needed five other men to go with him.

Shackleton chose the fittest men. They said a sad goodbye to their friends and they sailed away. Within half an hour the men were drenched. There was ice all over their beards and their clothes. The coldness made their bodies ache, and they knew that the pain would last for days.

After a fortnight the men began to look for land. One man stood up while the others hung onto him. Then, when the boat went up on a wave, he stared across the foaming sea. Sometimes the boat dived down again before he could have a proper look. Then he saw clearly. Yes, he could see the snow on the mountains!

The men were excited. They knew they were near South Georgia now.

Endurance trappe

They landed safely and they found a cave to shelter in. The whalers' village was over the mountains. Shackleton said that he and two others would go there for help. The rest of the men were too weak and ill for a difficult climb. They would have to wait until help arrived. There were thick sheets of ice on some of the mountains. In places the ice had dangerous cracks. They were so deep and wide that a man could fall down them and disappear. Snow-covered cracks were the worst of all because no one could see them.

The men reached the top of the mountains safely. Now they would have to go down a slope that was covered with ice. At first they tried cutting steps for themselves. However, this was far too slow. The sun was going down, and the cold at the top of the mountain could kill them. The men peered into the gloomy valley. Would it be safe to slide down the mountain or would they hit rocks? The men decided to risk their lives. Soon they were shooting over the ice on the seats of their trousers! They landed in snow — and they laughed till the mountains rang with the noise.

*Endurance* sails to Antarctic 1914

**South Georgia**
Boat arrives 10 May 1916

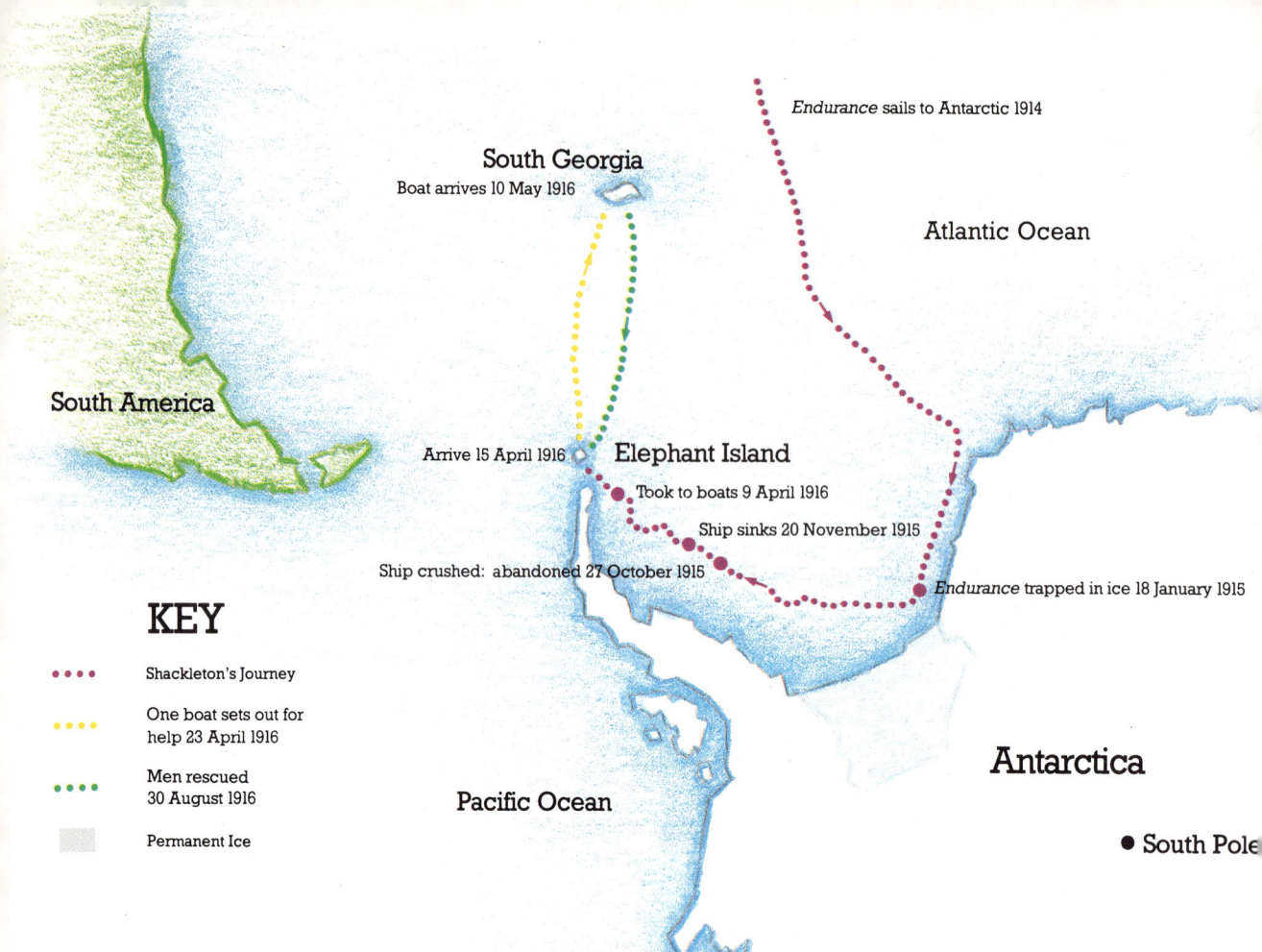

Atlantic Ocean

South America

Arrive 15 April 1916   **Elephant Island**
Took to boats 9 April 1916
Ship sinks 20 November 1915
Ship crushed: abandoned 27 October 1915
*Endurance* trapped in ice 18 January 1915

## KEY
• • • •  Shackleton's Journey
• • • •  One boat sets out for help 23 April 1916
• • • •  Men rescued 30 August 1916
▦  Permanent Ice

Pacific Ocean

Antarctica

• South Pole

They walked all night and at dawn they came to the whalers' village. Soon a ship set out to rescue the men on the other side of South Georgia. Another ship went to Elephant Island to rescue the twenty-two men who were there. They were all alive, but one man had lost his toes because of the terrible cold.

If you look at the map you can work out how many months they stayed on Elephant Island.